WORLD'S
WEIRDEST
SHARKS

Thanks to the creative team:
Senior Editor: Alice Peebles
Fact Checking: Tom Jackson
Picture Research: Nic Dean
Design: Perfect Bound Ltd

Hungry Tomato®
A division of Lerner Publishing Group, Inc.
241 First Avenue North
Minneapolis, MN 55401 USA

For reading levels and more information, look up this title at www.lernerbooks.com.

Main body text set in Scene Std Regular 10/13.
Typeface provided by Monotype Typography.

Library of Congress Cataloging-in-Publication Data

Names: Mason, Paul, 1967- author.
Title: World's weirdest sharks / Paul Mason.
Description: Minneapolis : Hungry Tomato, [2018] | Series: Wild world of sharks | Audience: Age 8-12. | Audience: Grade 4 to 6. | Includes index.
Identifiers: LCCN 2017026118| ISBN 9781512459760 (lb) | ISBN 9781512498783 (ebk pdf)
Subjects: LCSH: Sharks—Juvenile literature.
Classification: LCC QL638.9 .M293 2018 | DDC 597.3/3—dc23
LC record available at https://lccn.loc.gov/2017026118

Manufactured in the United States of America
2-46341-27704-7/2/2018

WORLD'S WEIRDEST SHARKS

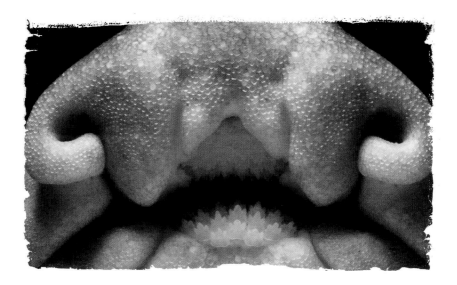

by Paul Mason

HUNGRY
TOMATO®
Minneapolis

CONTENTS

SHARKS: AMAZING ADAPTERS

There are around 450 different species of sharks. Between them, they can hunt almost everywhere. If an ocean contains prey, it will also have sharks hunting in it.

This strange-looking shark is called Stethacanthus. It lived during the Carboniferous Period, 359 to 299 million years ago.

Only males had the strange, anvil-shaped **dorsal fin**. It may have been a way to attract females, but no one is really sure.

Stethacanthus hunted in shallow coastal waters and ate fish and crustaceans.

Stethacanthus may have grown up to 6 feet (1.8 m) long, about the size of a whitetip reef shark.

Ancient Predators

Sharks have been on Earth for a long time—a really long time. The ancestors of today's sharks appeared about 450 million years ago. Compare this with humans. *Homo sapiens*, modern humans, first appeared less than 200,000 years ago. Sharks first spread through the world's oceans during the Carboniferous Period, so sharks ruled the oceans even before dinosaurs ruled Earth.

A Shark for Every Ocean

Over their long history, sharks have adapted to life in almost every ocean. These adaptations have given rise to some pretty weird creatures. You're about to meet some of the weirdest sharks of all.

Great white tooth

Megalodon tooth

The great white shark is the most feared shark in the ocean—but its extinct cousin Megalodon was roughly three times as long.

Great white shark

Megalodon

FRILLED SHARK

The frilled shark looks like something from a horror movie. With over 300 teeth, it's a good thing it only grows about 6 feet 6 inches (2 m) long and lives in the deep oceans.

DEEP-OCEAN HUNTER

The frilled shark has been recorded at depths over 1 mile (1.6 km) below the ocean surface. Light does not reach this far down, so the shark hunts in darkness. It likes upwellings, or places where cold, deep water moves upward. This is where plankton—and the fish that hunt the plankton—are common.

Old stories of sea serpents may have been based on frilled sharks. Sailors who caught one by accident would never have seen anything like it.

When it senses prey, the frilled shark strikes quickly.

AN ANCIENT SPECIES

The frilled shark rarely comes close to the surface, so few have ever been seen. In fact, this shark is so rare that it was only officially discovered in 2004. This is not a new shark species though. Scientists know it has been hunting in the deep oceans for at least 95 million years. Based on **fossil** evidence, some experts think it may have been down there for three times that long.

The frilled shark's most horrifying feature is its teeth.

As it strikes, the shark closes its gills, creating a suction effect that pulls prey toward its teeth.

Every row of teeth points back toward the shark's throat, making it almost impossible for prey to escape.

The shark's teeth are very white, which scientists think may attract squid and fish.

SHARK SCIENCE: BIG EATERS

Captured frilled sharks usually have little or nothing in their stomachs. This suggests that they probably do not eat often.

When frilled sharks do catch something, they eat large meals. There are folds of skin alongside the shark's stomach. These expand, allowing the shark to **digest** prey almost half its own size.

THRESHER SHARK

If you see a thresher shark coming toward you, you will probably think it is just an ordinary shark. If it turns sideways, though . . . wow! What a tail!

There are three different types of thresher shark: common, bigeye, and **pelagic**. Common threshers are the largest, followed by bigeye and pelagic.

This thresher shark is having tiny parasites picked off its skin by small fish.

Thresher sharks have weaker bites than most other sharks. They also have fewer teeth (usually 80, compared to a great white's 300). They do not rely on their jaws for catching prey.

Common and bigeye threshers are usually dark green or brown. They blend in with the ocean bottom as they swim along, hunting for prey. Pelagic threshers are usually bluish in color to blend in with the open ocean.

All threshers have large eyes, and the bigeye's are among the largest of all animals. A thresher's eyes point upward, enabling it to spot **schools** of fish swimming above.

THE LONGEST TAIL IN SHARKLAND

Compared to their overall size (up to 20 feet, or 6 m), these sharks have by far the longest tail in the shark world. A thresher's tail is its biggest weapon and can be half its total length. At nearly 10 feet (3 m), it matches the world's tallest-ever man, Robert Wadlow, who was 8 feet 11 inches (2.7 m) tall.

When the shark finds prey, it uses its tail like a whip, thrashing the water to stun and even kill fish.

SHARK SCIENCE: AN ORDER OF ODDBALLS

Scientists divide sharks into eight categories known as orders. Threshers are from the mackerel shark order.

Mackerel sharks have two dorsal fins, five gill slits, and a mouth that goes back past their eyes. Apart from that, they do not always have much in common. Mackerel sharks include threshers and goblin sharks as well as megamouth and basking sharks.

GOBLIN SHARK

The goblin shark hunts in the deep ocean more than
half a mile below the surface. The sun's light does
not reach this far down. But the goblin does not
need light to hunt.

A Nose for Prey

At 10–13 feet (3–4 m) long, the goblin shark is a scary sight. It has
a long, flat snout that sticks out in front of its head like a sword
laid flat. This is its secret weapon. The snout acts like a metal
detector, but instead of detecting metal, it picks up electricity.

The snout is so sensitive that it can pick up 1/10,000,000th of
a volt. It easily detects the tiny amounts of electricity produced
by the goblin's prey. Crabs, fish, squid, and other creatures have
nowhere to hide—even if they bury themselves on the sea bottom,
the goblin shark will sniff them out.

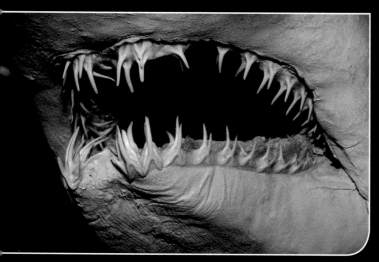

High-Speed Jaws

Once it senses prey, the
goblin shark strikes in the
blink of an eye. Other sharks
race forward with their whole
body to grab a victim—not
the goblin shark, though.
Its jaws alone push out
from under its nose at high
speed, grabbing its victim.
Once caught, the prey is not
likely to escape the shark's
needle-sharp teeth.

The goblin shark's mouth is full of snaggly teeth,
which make it difficult for their prey to wriggle free.

A goblin shark cruises the ocean floor, looking for prey buried in the sandy bottom.

SHARK SCIENCE:
AMPULLAE OF LORENZINI

The ampullae of Lorenzini are pores in a shark's snout that allows the shark to sense the electric field of its prey. The pores are filled with gel and lined with cells that can sense tiny vibrations. Any electrical pulse in the water, such as the electrical pulse of a heartbeat, is felt by the cells. This signals to the shark that there is something alive right under its nose.

WHALE SHARK

The whale shark is the biggest shark in the ocean. In fact, it is the biggest fish of any kind. Despite its huge size, the whale shark is harmless to all but the smallest sea creatures.

The whale shark is (much) bigger than a bus.

The biggest whale sharks are 40 feet (12 m) long—almost the length of a double-decker bus. They weigh about 11 tons (10 metric tonnes), which is the same as five rhinoceroses.

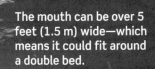

The mouth can be over 5 feet (1.5 m) wide—which means it could fit around a double bed.

PLANKTON AND KRILL

The whale shark swims along with its mouth open, sucking up plankton and krill. These tiny creatures are one of the building blocks of ocean life. They are at the bottom of the **food chain**. Without them, animals higher up the food chain could not survive. This makes whale sharks an indicator of the health of the oceans. If there is plenty of plankton for them to eat, other creatures will have enough to eat too.

A CRAFTY HUNTER

Whale sharks are crafty and patient. They have been seen waiting for hours until fish eggs hatch, then swooping in and gulping down all of the young. Whale sharks migrate from place to place, depending on where they can find food. They have been tracked making enormous journeys of more than 7,500 miles (12,000 km).

A shark this big could be a terrifying predator. It's a good thing a whale shark's main prey is plankton, krill, and small fish.

SHARK SCIENCE:
WHALE SHARK FINGERPRINTS

Sharks do not have fingerprints, of course—they do not even have fingers. But every whale shark still has its own personal ID.

Whale sharks all have a pattern of spots and stripes on their backs. No two sharks have exactly the same pattern. Scientists use the patterns to identify different sharks and track their movements.

SAW SHARK

The saw shark is a weird-looking shark indeed. Its saw is so long that it looks as though it would get in the way of feeding rather than helping the shark catch prey.

HUNTING TECHNIQUE

A saw shark's prey consists of small fish, **crustaceans,** and squid. The shark hunts in shallow water near the coast, such as bays and **estuaries**. The saw shark begins its hunt by searching for the tiny electrical signals of its prey's heartbeat. Once it senses them, it knows there is something buried in the sand.

This Japanese saw shark is a little over 3 feet 3 inches (1 m) long. It hunts prey on the sandy seabed.

KILLING PREY

Once the saw shark detects prey, its saw swings into action. The shark sweeps it quickly back and forth. No matter if the prey tries to escape or stays where it is, it gets sliced up. The shark gobbles down the stunned, injured, or dead fish.

Sensors under the shark's saw detect tiny electrical charges given off by hidden fish.

Some sensors detect tiny movements in the water.

Long, whiskery barbels contain touch- and smell-sensitive cells, allowing the shark to feel and sniff out prey.

SHARK SCIENCE: BABY SAW SHARKS

When baby longnose sawsharks are born, their teeth are folded back into their snouts. This prevents the baby sharks' mother from being cut to pieces while she is giving birth. Within hours, the babies' longest teeth have sprung forward, ready for action. Smaller teeth then begin to grow between the long ones.

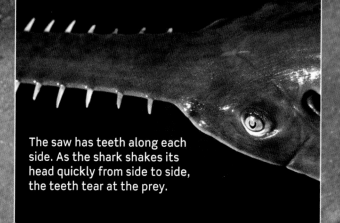

The saw has teeth along each side. As the shark shakes its head quickly from side to side, the teeth tear at the prey.

HORN SHARK

The horn shark belongs to a group called bullhead sharks. These get their name from their large, square-shaped heads that look like they could give you a nasty headbutt!

The horn shark is named after the hornlike ridges above its eyes.

Some horn sharks eat so many purple sea urchins that their teeth are dyed purple.

For its size, about 3 feet 3 inches (1 m), this shark has one of the most powerful bites in the animal world. This is very useful for crushing hard-shelled prey.

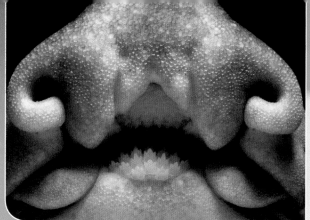

Small, hooked front teeth grab prey. Larger, flat side teeth grind up food.

HUNTING AND HIDING

Despite appearances, the horn shark is not likely to be aggressive in any way. In fact it is very shy and mostly stays within a small home territory.

The horn shark hunts at night and hides in a cave or a crevice during the day. It usually has a favorite hiding place. After a night of hunting, it returns to the same spot, day after day, for years.

This shark does not like light at all. If you shine a bright light on one at night, it usually sinks to the bottom and lies there without moving, pretending not to exist.

BOTTOM WALKER

Mollusks, crustaceans, starfish, and sea urchins make up the horn shark's diet. It is not a great swimmer, so instead of swimming, it uses its **pectoral fins** to walk along the bottom as it looks for food.

SHARK SCIENCE: HORN SHARK BREEDING

Horn sharks do not give birth to live young. They lay cone-shaped eggs. The female wedges her eggs into tight spaces in the rocky sea bottom. This makes it difficult for predators to find and eat the eggs before the baby horn sharks have hatched.

EPAULETTE SHARK

If there's one thing most people really do not want to hear, it's that some sharks can walk on land. But at least one shark can do just that.

Rock-Pool Hunting

The epaulette shark lives in shallow water near coral reefs. As the **tide** drops, parts of the reef are left exposed to the air. Rock pools are formed, and these are where the epaulette shark hunts. The fish trapped in the pools are unable to escape to sea until the tide rises again. They are easy pickings for the shark.

Reef-Crawler

The epaulette's plan is to be left in a rock pool with a lot of tasty fish. But sometimes the plan goes wrong. The shark miscalculates and finds itself stranded on the dry reef. When this happens, the epaulette can use its strong pectoral fins to crawl across the reef to water. If the distance is too far, the shark lies still and waits for the tide to rise again.

Like the horn shark, the epaulette shark moves around partly by crawling along the sea floor using its pectoral fins.

Epaulettes sometimes eat crustaceans. When they do, their sharp teeth flatten and become shell-crushing plates.

The shark's epaulettes are just about where its shoulders would be—if sharks had shoulders.

An epaulette is a decoration on the shoulder of a jacket. The epaulette shark gets its name from the black spot on its side.

Epaulette sharks are common in the seas around Australia's Great Barrier Reef.

SHARK SCIENCE:
A FISH OUT OF WATER

Sharks are a kind of fish, and fish need to be in water to breathe. So how does the epaulette shark survive when it is stranded on a dry reef?

The answer is that the shark powers down its brain and slows its heart rate and breathing. This means it uses far less oxygen. As a result, epaulettes can survive 60 times longer without oxygen than a human can.

GHOST SHARK

When is a shark not a shark? When it's a ghost shark! Technically, a ghost shark is not a shark at all. It's a chimera.

The ghost shark hunts in the deep ocean, haunting the depths where light never reaches.

This long tail gave ghost sharks one of their other names: ratfish.

CHIMERAS AND SHARKS

Chimeras and sharks are close relatives. Both have a skeleton made of tough cartilage instead of bone. And they look alike. Ghost sharks look most similar to sharks from the bullhead order such as the horn shark.

Flat plates in the mouth grind up mollusks found on the seabed.

Large pectoral fins are used for swimming.

FRANKENSHARK

Some types of ghost shark look
like a sharky Frankenstein's
monster, a creature
stitched together by a
scientist. Along their
heads are lines with dots running alongside
like stitches. These are thought to be sensors
for locating prey. This shark's blue-grey color
also looks spooky as it swims through the
deep ocean.

GHOST-SHARK HUNTING

Ghost sharks are rare and even taking photos
of them is a tricky job. The sharks live in the
deepest part of the ocean, and there are
hardly any around. You could wait underwater
for weeks before one swam by. In 2009 a crew
filming life on the sea bottom caught a ghost
shark on camera—but only by accident!

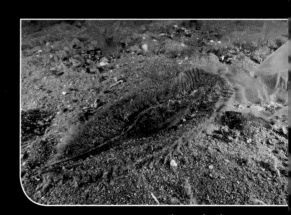

Ghost shark egg

SHARK SCIENCE: CHIMERAS

How do sharks differ from chimeras? One
obvious difference is that instead of having
teeth like a true shark, chimeras have toothy
plates in their mouths. Unlike a shark's teeth,
these plates are not replaced again and again
throughout the ghost shark's life.

Chimeras also swim mainly using their
pectoral fins like wings while a shark swishes its
tail from side to side to move through the water.

WOBBEGONG

This shark's extraordinary appearance makes it an effective hunter. It waits patiently on the seabed, and when unwary food swims by, it strikes like lightning!

None of the little fish in this school have spotted the wobbegong they are swimming past!

The wobbegong's sharp teeth are shaped so that anything it bites cannot wriggle away. Once a wobbegong grabs hold, it does not like to let go.

A wide, flat body is perfect for hiding on the sea floor and pretending to be a rock.

MASTERS OF DISGUISE

In the shark world, the master of disguise is the wobbegong. There are twelve different kinds of wobbegong. All are camouflaged brown, grey, and yellow, making them almost impossible to spot on the sea bottom. Some have frills around their jaws that look just like seaweed. To a fish looking for shelter, or perhaps some food to nibble, these frills look welcome— right up until the wobbegong pounces!

ACCIDENTAL ATTACKER

Unfortunately, it's not only fish that find wobbegongs hard to spot. Around Australia's busy coastline, people sometimes accidentally tread on a wobbegong that's lying disguised on the bottom. Sometimes the shark just swims off, but once in a while it bites back.

SHARK SCIENCE: SMALL EATERS

Wobbegongs need to eat only once every three or four days. Since they do not swim much, their bodies do not need a lot of energy from food. So wobbegongs have developed with a slow **metabolism**.

The dangling frills are called dermal lobes. They are part of the wobbengong's disguise, and they also attract prey.

GREENLAND SHARK

The Greenland shark is one of the longest-lived creatures on Earth. It can easily survive up to 200 years. Some are thought to have reached double that age!

ARCTIC HUNTER

This shark lives in the cold seas of the Subarctic. It swims to depths where sunlight never reaches. It grows as large as a pickup truck and is a fearsome hunter. Though the shark mostly eats fish, it is also thought to attack seals and small whales. Greenland sharks have even been seen grabbing reindeer and other animals that come too close to the edge of the ice.

The Greenland shark is one of the world's largest sharks. At over 20 feet (6 m) long, it is similar in size to the great white shark.

ADAPTED FOR THE COLD

The Greenland shark is specially adapted to life in the coldest seas. Though able to make short bursts of speed, it is usually slow-moving. As the temperature drops, the shark moves more and more slowly. The shark is not quite hibernating because it never stops swimming. Rather, it is shutting down its body as much as possible to save energy in the cold.

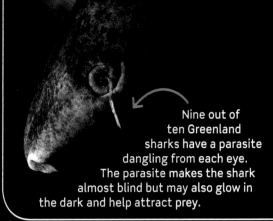

Nine out of ten Greenland sharks have a parasite dangling from **each eye**. The parasite makes the shark almost blind but may **also glow** in the dark and help attract prey.

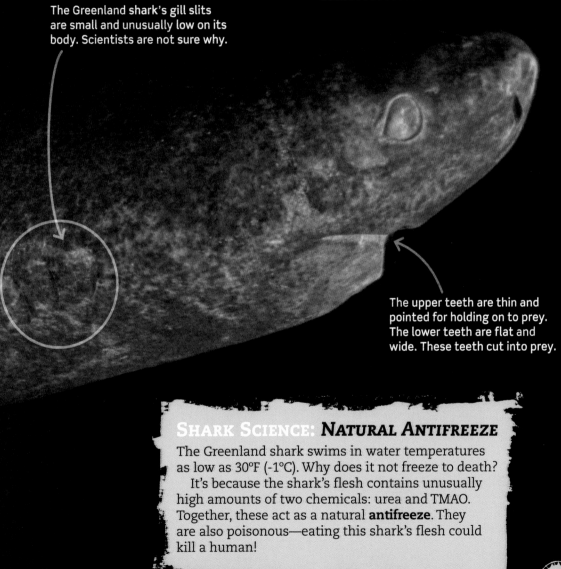

The Greenland shark's gill slits are small and unusually low on its body. Scientists are not sure why.

The upper teeth are thin and pointed for holding on to prey. The lower teeth are flat and wide. These teeth cut into prey.

SHARK SCIENCE: NATURAL ANTIFREEZE

The Greenland shark swims in water temperatures as low as 30°F (-1°C). Why does it not freeze to death?

It's because the shark's flesh contains unusually high amounts of two chemicals: urea and TMAO. Together, these act as a natural **antifreeze**. They are also poisonous—eating this shark's flesh could kill a human!

SEVEN INCREDIBLE SHARK FACTS

1 ONE SHARK, TWO NAMES

Young zebra sharks have black-edged white stripes down their sides (which is why they are called zebra sharks). But as the sharks get older, the pattern changes to become more spotty. The sharks are then sometimes called leopard sharks.

2 FEMALE SHARKS CAN REPRODUCE WITHOUT MALE SHARKS

It is incredibly rare, but female sharks in an aquarium have been known to reproduce alone. The young are healthy but do not reproduce their own baby sharks.

3 HORN SHARKS ARE NOT BIG TRAVELERS

Horn sharks are not very good swimmers, so perhaps it's no surprise that they do not like to travel far. They usually stay within a 0.4-square-mile (1 km²) area. The farthest a horn shark has ever been known to swim is 10 miles (16 km)!

4 GREENLAND SHARKS LIVE A REALLY LONG TIME

In 2010–2013, scientists investigated the ages of Greenland sharks. The largest one they caught was thought to be between 272 and 512 years old. This means it could have been alive at the time of Columbus's final voyage of exploration in 1502.

5 MEGALODON LIVES! NOT. . .

No one knows exactly why Megalodon died out. In fact, some people will tell you it did not. They say there could still be these ancient sharks swimming in the deep oceans. The only trouble is no one has actually seen one, and there is no evidence to support the idea!

6 SOME SHARKS GLOW IN THE DARK

Swell sharks live about 1,600 feet (500 m) below the surface. They are shy and are rarely seen—at least by humans. But the sharks have a substance in their skin that glows and is visible to other swell sharks.

7 SHARKS HAD A GOLDEN AGE

The Carboniferous Period of Earth's prehistory is sometimes called the Golden Age of Sharks. This is when sharks first spread widely through our oceans. Experts think there may have been thousands of different kinds of shark at this time.

SHARK EXTREMES

Sharks come in many different shapes and sizes. They range in size from enormous to tiny. They live in deep oceans and shallow waters, far out to sea and in rivers. Here are just a few extremes of the shark world.

BIGGEST

The biggest shark—and the world's biggest fish—is the whale shark. The largest recorded specimen was 43 feet (13 m) long. The second biggest is the basking shark which can reach more than 30 feet (9 m) long.

FASTEST

The fastest shark is the shortfin mako. Measuring how fast a shark is traveling in the open ocean is difficult, but some say that makos can swim at over 43 miles per hour (70 km/h)—plenty fast enough to break the speed limit in most cities.

DEEPEST

The cow shark (also called the bluntnose sixgill shark) is an amazingly adaptable hunter. Young cow sharks sometimes hunt in very shallow water, but adults have been found as far down as 8,200 feet (2,500 m). Other deep-sea sharks include goblin, ghost, and frilled sharks.

MOST DANGEROUS

The most dangerous shark, based on statistics from the Florida Museum of Natural History in the United States, is the great white shark. By 2017 great whites were thought to have killed at least 80 people since records began in 1580. Next came tiger sharks (31 people) and bull sharks (27 people).

HOTTEST

Scientists got a shock when they sent an underwater camera down off the coast of Fiji to view an active undersea volcano. Among the creatures swimming around inside the volcano's crater were two kinds of shark: scalloped hammerheads and silky sharks. They would not survive an actual eruption but were able to swim in the ashy, acidic water.

SMALLEST

The dwarf lanternshark grows to no more than 8.3 inches (21 cm)—about as long as a grown-up's hand. It lives in deep, dark waters off the coast of South America. The shark gets its name from being bioluminescent: it glows in the dark as a way of attracting food.

GLOSSARY

antifreeze

liquid that stops another liquid from freezing solid

crustacean

an animal such as a crab, lobster, or shrimp with a shell and jointed limbs

digest

to break down food so that it can be used by the body

dorsal fin

a fin on a fish's back

estuary

a wide, shallow area of salty water where a river meets the sea

food chain

a series of living things in which each animal depends on the next as a source of food

fossil

the remains of an ancient plant or animal contained in rock

metabolism

the chemical workings of the body, such as food digestion

mollusk

an animal such as a snail, mussel, or octopus with a soft body inside a hard shell

pectoral fin

a fin on the sides of a fish's body

pelagic

inhabiting the deep, open ocean, a long way from land

pore

a tiny opening in the skin

school

a large group of the same kind of fish swimming together

tide

the rise and fall in the level of the sea, which happens regularly twice a day

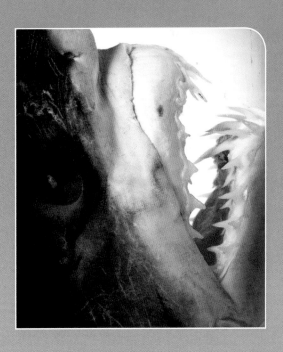

INDEX

ABOUT THE AUTHOR

Paul Mason is a prolific author of children's books, many award-nominated, on such subjects as ways to save the planet, vile things that go wrong with the body, and the world's craziest inventors. His books are filled with surprising, unbelievable, or just plain revolting facts. Mason lives at a secret location on the coast of Europe, where his writing shack usually smells of drying wetsuit (he's a former international swimmer and a keen surfer).

Picture Credits
(abbreviations: t = top; b = bottom; c = center;
l = left; r = right)
© Alamy Stock Photo: Arco Images GmbH 21r; Bill
Bachman 17b; Brandon Cole 30l; David Fleetham 28l; Erik
Schlogl 18; Ivy Close Images 8bl; Jeff Rotman 11t; Juergen
Freund 25t; Kelvin Aitken / VWPics 1, 7tr; 8, 12; 12bl, 16;
louise murray 27tr; Martin Strmiska 30b; Nature Picture
Librar 10, 22, 23t; Solvin Zankl 9tr; Stocktrek Images, Inc.
6, 7r; The Natural History Museum 31br; WaterFrame 10l,
23r, 24, 26, 28b.
© FLPA: Fred Bavendam/Minden Pictures 28t; Jeffrey
Rotman/Biosphoto 3; Oliver Lucanus/Minden Pictures 20;
Peter Verhoog/Minden Pictures 2; Reinhard Dirscherl 14bl;
Tim Fitzharris/Minden Pictures 4.
© www.shutterstock.com: David Evison 14.